Anger Management Workbook for Kids

50+ Fun and Engaging Activities to Help Children Regain Control and Become Calmer and Happier

Michael B. Stump
The Mentor Bucket

Table of Contents

Introduction

Sometimes we all have moments when we feel as though we are going to burst because some things happen outside of our bodies that we cannot control. These big emotions form for many reasons. Sometimes we feel unhappy at the way other people treat us. We begin to get frustrated and upset, and we make mistakes in the way we behave. There can be all sorts of unexpected unknowns or other factors.

These factors can increase our feelings, and if we don't learn how to manage them, the emotions can turn into bigger issues.

Anger can turn into crying, yelling, frustration, anxiety, and more.

We are all responsible for our emotions.

That is the first lesson everyone has to learn.

When we don't learn these lessons, life can get harder.

Children do not come into this world knowing how to handle these emotions. They require safe spaces, protection, and unconditional love from those raising them and teaching them life lessons. When they get the right idea about feelings—whether positive or negative—and how to handle these emotions, they can grow into amazing adults with a refined view of the world. They will also develop an empathetic perspective and can help others around them.

Emotions are not bad or good. They just are. Children feel emotions just as powerfully as adults do. Things can spiral downward quickly when they don't know how to work with what they are feeling.

That is what this workbook is for.

We have written this book to help you and your child learn how emotions work, why emotions are there, what triggers the emotions, and what you can do to help yourself and the children in your life develop healthy tools and outlets for any angry feelings that come their way.

The methods in this workbook will take consistency and practice to apply if they're to work effectively, but soon you'll start to see your little one deploy the tools and techniques without being told. You'll feel a sense of satisfaction and pride in knowing that you've done everything that you can for your child.

Let's get started!

A Letter for Grown-Ups

Hello, Grown-ups!

It's great that you've picked up a workbook to help explain what anger is and how to help your children manage it. Being responsible for small humans is one of the hardest things you will ever do in your life, but it comes with so many rewards and so much love that the hard work you put into helping your tiny people is worth every ounce of energy you've put in.

You're here to help them learn how to maneuver in the world.

We're here to help you know how to do that.

Anger can get out of control very quickly, especially when your children cannot express what they feel or why they feel it.

We present this book to you to help you gain new knowledge and an excellent understanding of how to model healthy behaviors for children. You are doing an amazing job - especially on the days that things get hard! We all make mistakes and learn from them. You can provide every opportunity for your child to learn how to be an adult in the healthiest way possible.

You are doing a fantastic job.

When using this book, you can work on it in several ways.

1. You can work together on this book with your child.

2. Your child can work independently from time to time, but also make sure that they tell you about what they learned. That way, they know you're involved.

3. You can let your child read the book to you, and then, they can do the exercises alone.

Doing activities together can create a wonderful bond with you and your children. They can see that you model patience when they make mistakes and that you are interested in every aspect of their life. However, having your child work independently at times is important, as well. They will have the opportunity to learn how to be self-sufficient and find tools specific to them.

If you get frustrated, or if they get frustrated at some point during this workbook, know that it's okay to walk away from it for a time. The whole point of this book is to form healthy habits and innovative tools when anger comes along. Taking a break is a good thing, and it doesn't press kids when they are already feeling anxious.

Keep up the great work!

Michael B. Stump

A Letter for Kids

Hi, Kids!

Did you know that emotions are part of being a human? You will feel all kinds of feelings every day, and anger is one of those feelings. But just because anger feels bad doesn't mean it is a "bad" feeling.

There are actually no good or bad emotions, but there are some positive and negative ways you can react to those emotions. And this workbook is going to help you figure out how to respond in the best possible ways when you do feel angry.

Did you know that the anger emotion is telling you something when you feel it?

It can tell you that you don't like how something happened. Anger can also signal frustration, hunger, sleepiness, fear, and many other things you may not realize. This workbook will help you figure out the WHY of your anger too.

You cannot control the emotions that you have. They signal all types of things that are going on in your body and how you feel about what is going on in the real world. Emotions are an important part of being a human!

You are responsible for your actions. Each time you act out on emotion, it does affect other people around you. If you are happy and you hug someone, they feel that love. Just the same, if you are angry and you throw something, they get hurt too!

You are an amazing kid, and we know you don't want to hurt anyone with your actions.

This workbook will help give you the tools to make sure that you keep treating people, and yourself, in the best way possible, even when you are feeling yucky because of anger.

We look forward to helping you, and we can't wait to get started!

Michael B. Stump

Hello, Anger

What is Anger?

There can be a lot of questions when you are feeling big emotions. Everyone has a lot of emotions, even you! You can be happy, grumpy, sad, jealous, and more. Anger is also an emotion you can have, and there are probably times when you feel like you want to explode, and so you do.

Those explosions happen because you don't understand how to release your anger positively; instead, you may feel guilty, sad, and even tired after you erupt.

This section is going to help you understand what anger is, how to describe it, and how to tell that your anger is starting to boil over.

This section is also going to tell you that being angry is okay! We ALL feel mad at times, and when you do, it's important to know why you are feeling it.

Where Does Anger Come From?

There are a lot of things that might make you angry, and there are different types of anger too. The point of this book will be to help you decode what kind of anger you are feeling and why you are feeling it so much. Anger does come from inside of you, and it is an alarm that tells you that something isn't quite right in the world around you.

There are many reasons that anger can happen. You can get mad at other people. You can get mad at yourself. You can get mad at a video game, the weather, the dinner you are eating, and more. There are LOTS of reasons you can get angry, and these can happen every day if you're not careful.

One of the best ways to help you learn how to react well to your anger is to know when you are angry. And this section is going to help you figure that out.

EXERCISE 1:
How Do You Show & Feel Anger?

Directions: Check off items that seem familiar when you're feeling mad or angry

- Heavy breathing.
- Hands are in a "fist."
- Heart feels like it is racing.
- Face is red.
- Eyes are squinched.
- Nose is flaring.
- Muscles are tight.
- Teeth are clenched together.
- You want to scream.
- Your chest feels like a balloon ready to pop.
- Your thoughts are racing.
- You want to throw something.
- You want to kick something.
- You want to hit something.
- You just want to "run away."
- You want to say something mean to hurt someone else.
- You don't like the way you feel.
- You want to push someone over.
- You just want to destroy something.
- You immediately hate your life.
- You immediately hate someone else.
- You say something bad about yourself (example: "I am so stupid!)
- You immediately don't like yourself.
- You see the color red.
- You see the color white.

- You feel the color red.
- You feel the color white.
- You just want to push something over.
- You scream into a pillow.
- You pull something apart.
- You want to hit yourself.
- You want to hurt yourself.
- You want to rip something up.
- You have a hard time catching your breath.
- You have a hard time seeing straight.
- You don't want to do anything with anyone.
- You don't want to do anything at all.
- You just feel "done" with everything.
- You want to cry.
- You do cry.
- You yell.

Fill in other things not mentioned below.

_____

_____

_____

_____

_____

Once you know how you look, act, and feel when you are angry, you'll be able to see it coming much easier! Now you can figure out some other things with the next EXERCISEs.

EXERCISE 2:
Anger Detective Time to Figure Out the WHY, WHERE, and WHAT of Your Anger

Directions: There are some questions to ask yourself when you get angry. It will help you figure out where your anger came from, why you are so mad, and what you can do to make yourself feel better. Circle the possible answers OR fill in the answers on the blank spots.

Question 1: Why am I mad?

I lost a game.

I woke up late.

I didn't sleep well.

My sister or brother said something mean.

My brother or sister did something mean.

I made a mistake.

I dropped something.

I broke something by accident.

I don't want to do something.

I don't like what happened at school.

My teacher said something to me in front of the class.

My parents corrected me in front of my friends.

I am embarrassed about something.

_____

_____

_____

_____

_____

_____

_____

Question 2:
Where did my anger start? — Look for clues

Think about where your anger came from. Sometimes when you get angry, it can be a mystery. Before you react to your anger, look back during your day to find out where your anger started. Answer the questions below to help you find clues to what led you to get so mad.

Think Where did it start? (fill in your answers on the lines)

Did you sleep well? _____

Are you tired now? _____

Did you eat a good breakfast? _____

What did you eat? _____

Do you think you ate enough good food? _____

What did you eat for lunch? _____

Did you eat enough good food? _____

Are you hungry now? _____

Did something happen when you were getting ready for the day?

_____

Did something happen during the start of your day?

_____

_____

Did something happen in the middle of your day? _____

_____

_____

Did something happen toward the end of your day? _____

_____

_____

Did someone do something that you didn't like? _____

If you answered 'Yes' to the question above, describe what happened, what didn't you like? How did it make you feel?

_____

_____

_____

_____

Did something not go as planned? If so, what was it? How did it go? How was it supposed to go?

_____

_____

_____

_____

_____

What are some things that annoy you? _____

_____

_____

Did any of the things that annoy you happen to you today?

_____

_____

_____

_____

Did you do poorly on a test? _____

Did you answer questions in school wrong? _____

Did someone blame you for something? _____

Did something embarrassing happen? _____

Did you lose a game? _____

Did you lose something special to you? _____

Did someone say something mean to you? _____

Do you have to do something you don't want to do? If so, what?

_____

_____

_____

Finally, write about your day. Remember to add anything, even small clues, to let you be the detective of your emotions.

_____

_____

_____

_____

_____

_____

_____

_____

_____

_____

_____

_____

_____

_____

_____

_____

Now, you should have an idea of where your anger started, write down what you detected and solve your mystery!

_____

_____

_____

_____

_____

_____

_____

_____

_____

_____

_____

_____

_____

_____

_____

_____

Question 3:
What could make me feel better?

Now that your anger mystery is solved, it's time to find some helpful tips to make you feel better. Circle the activities that seem like something you would be interested in. And if you don't see any ideas that you like, fill in some other items in the blank lines on the next page.

- Eat a healthy snack.
- Color in a coloring book.
- Go for a walk outside.
- Clean your room.
- Play basketball.
- Play baseball.
- Play football.
- Go for a run.
- Hit golf balls.
- Kick soccer balls.

Take a break — lie on the bed or sit on your bedroom floor and take some time out for yourself.

- Listen to music.
- Read a book.
- Draw a picture.
- Paint a picture.
- Write a story.
- Watch a movie.
- Bake a cake.
- Dance.
- Watch sports.
- Play a game.
- Play a video game.

- Take a nap.
- Knit.
- Sew.
- Crochet.
- Make a vision board for your future.
- Learn something new.
- Build a birdhouse.
- Paint the birdhouse.
- Walk the dog.
- Volunteer.
- Help a neighbor.
- Mow the lawn.
- Work in the garden.
- Do some other yard work.
- Make a smoothie.

OTHER OPTIONS:

_____

_____

_____

_____

_____

_____

_____

_____

EXERCISE 3:
Hello Anger

Did you know that there are different kinds of anger? One of the best things you can do for yourself is to figure out what kind of anger you are feeling.

Find the different words that mean anger in the Word Search below. Circle the words when you find them. After you find all the words, you can name your anger by answering a few questions.

Name Your Anger

D	I	T	N	E	I	T	A	P	M	I	L	L	E
I	A	T	A	L	I	T	D	T	E	E	F	U	V
S	N	E	A	F	E	E	C	X	T	S	T	F	I
T	T	P	E	M	N	R	C	D	E	R	L	T	M
R	E	W	P	R	A	I	O	E	E	O	E	N	A
A	N	E	U	N	T	W	A	N	N	O	Y	E	D
U	R	B	K	A	N	Y	P	M	U	R	G	S	E
G	A	Y	B	B	A	R	C	T	O	F	D	E	F
H	G	L	D	A	G	I	T	A	T	E	D	R	E
T	E	I	N	L	O	F	F	E	N	D	E	D	A
E	D	G	I	D	F	U	R	I	O	U	S	D	T
I	R	V	R	E	S	E	N	T	I	N	G	E	E
Y	I	N	M	I	R	R	I	T	A	B	L	E	D
D	I	S	A	P	P	O	I	N	T	E	D	A	R

EXCITABLE
TEMPER
AGITATED
OFFENDED
DEFEATED
DISTRAUGHT
DISAPPOINTED
RESENTFUL
RESENTING
FURIOUS
IMPATIENT
GRUMPY
IRRITABLE
ANNOYED
CRABBY
BURNED
LET DOWN
ENRAGED
LIVID
CRANKY
MAD
ANGRY

Play this puzzle online at : https://thewordsearch.com/puzzle/3311642/

Naming Your Anger

Before you can name what anger you are feeling, you'll have to define it first.

When did you first realize you were angry?

_____

What set your anger off?

_____

What does your anger do?

_____

What does your anger tell you to do?

_____

Is your anger loud?

_____

Is your anger quiet?

_____

Can you ignore your anger?

_____

Do you have to listen to the anger?

_____

If you do something new do you feel better?

_____

NOW What kind of anger are you feeling? _____

_____

EXERCISE 4:
What Does Your Anger Look Like?

It's time to draw your anger out. What does your anger look like?

Directions: Things to think about when drawing your anger — think about the color, smell, and shape. Does your anger have a face? What does it look like? If your anger has legs, how does it stand? What other features does your anger have (fists, eyebrows, growl-face, etc.)?

EXERCISE 5:
Blame Game

When you get angry, sometimes it's easy to blame other people, but remember, you are responsible for your actions—even if you cannot control your emotions, you do not have to act or blame others. When you're upset, think about who you would want to blame and then reframe your words to get rid of that blame game.

Directions: Think about when you get angry—is the immediate reaction that you want to blame someone? Write down that "blame" on the lines and rewrite it with different words to remove the "blame."

Example:

BLAMING: Tobi told me to do it!

REFRAMING: I knew it was wrong when Tobi said something about it, but I did it anyway.

Now you try!

BLAMING: _____

_____

REFRAMING: _____

_____

BLAMING: _____

_____

REFRAMING: _____

_____

BLAMING: _____

_____

REFRAMING: _____

_____

BLAMING: _____

_____

REFRAMING: _____

_____

BLAMING: _____

_____

REFRAMING: _____

_____

BLAMING: _____

_____

REFRAMING: _____

_____

_____

_____

BLAMING: _____

_____

REFRAMING: _____

_____

BLAMING: _____

_____

REFRAMING: _____

_____

BLAMING: _____

_____

REFRAMING: _____

_____

BLAMING: _____

_____

REFRAMING: _____

_____

_____

_____

EXERCISE 6:
You're Responsible for Your Feelings

Like the EXERCISE above, you have to be responsible for your feelings and actions. You cannot control your emotions, but you are responsible for them. Only you can stop yourself from acting negatively. Also, when you can, take your feelings and look at them differently; you can turn your experience into a growing moment (which is amazing for you!).

Directions: Think about the last time you were angry. How could you have taken responsibility for it? Take one line and describe how you got mad and what happened with your anger, then on the next line, write down how you took responsibility for it. If you didn't take responsibility for your anger, write about how you COULD HAVE taken responsibility instead.

Example:

ANGER: Tobi made me angry because she took my toy. She made me scream because she wouldn't give it back to me.

RESPONSIBILITY: I am responsible for my anger. I got angry when Tobi took my toy. I did not have to scream at Tobi when I was angry.

Now you try!

ANGER: _____

_____

RESPONSIBILITY: _____

_____

_____

_____

ANGER: _____

_____

RESPONSIBILITY: _____

_____

ANGER: _____

_____

RESPONSIBILITY: _____

_____

ANGER: _____

_____

RESPONSIBILITY: _____

_____

ANGER: _____

_____

RESPONSIBILITY: _____

_____

_____

_____

ANGER: _____

_____

RESPONSIBILITY: _____

_____

ANGER: _____

_____

RESPONSIBILITY: _____

_____

ANGER: _____

_____

RESPONSIBILITY: _____

_____

ANGER: _____

_____

RESPONSIBILITY: _____

_____

_____

_____

EXERCISE 7:
Turn Your Mistakes Around—Mirror Your Lessons

When we make mistakes, we can get angry or feel embarrassed. But, the great thing about making mistakes is you can learn something new about yourself.

Directions: On side A, talk about your mistake. On side B, write or draw what you learned from the error. You can learn many things! You could know what to do the next time a similar mistake happens. You can learn how to own up to your mistake. You can learn what NOT to do. And, you can learn how to make a mistake right along with many other lessons that you can come up with.

Example:

Side A: I yelled at my mom because I didn't want to clean up my mess. Then, when she gave me my consequence, I got so angry I kicked the chair over. The noise was loud and scared me, but I ran away screaming instead of picking it up.

Side B: I learned a few things. a) If I cleaned up my mess in the first place, none of the other things would have happened. b) Yelling at my mom was wrong, and I didn't feel good doing it. c) Screaming when the chair hit the floor did not help me feel better. I felt worse after I ran away. d) Next time, I will try to clean up my mess. If I don't or I can't, I can talk to my mom about WHY I need help. e) If I feel like yelling or screaming, I can stop and take a breath and not let the yelling come out of my mouth. f) I should never kick or hit anything when I'm angry. If I'm angry, talking about it with my mom will help me feel better than yelling, screaming, kicking, or hitting.

Side A	Side B

Side A	Side B

EXERCISE 8:
Write it Out

Did you know that your thoughts can become angry when you start to feel angry too?

Getting your emotions and thoughts out of your head and heart helps you feel better. But, instead of acting out your feelings and thoughts, try writing them out. You can write out your mad thoughts and your angry emotions below, but to keep up the practice, you can also have your grown-ups get you an "Anger Journal" that you can write in any time you start to get mad.

You can also write daily about small things that might make you angry.

As a bonus, you can write down ways to help yourself and how you can react each time you get mad.

Example:

Today did NOT go well. I was late getting up to go to school, and, instead of getting to eat breakfast, I had to search for my shoes. They were NOT in the right place. EVERYTHING WENT WRONG THIS MORNING. I feel like growling or yelling. I wanted this morning to go better. Now I am worried that everything will be messed up for the day. I just want to feel not mad and don't know how!

NOW YOU TRY BELOW:

_____

_____

_____

_____

_____

EXERCISE 9:
How Your Body Lets You Know You're Angry

Directions: Write a list of how YOU react to anger. Then draw a picture of yourself (you can draw the picture of yourself looking either happy or sad, no matter what you draw, just have fun doing it!).

How Does My Body Get Angry?

Examples:
clenched teeth, red face, scrunched eyebrows.

EXERCISE 10:
How Your Brain Reacts to Anger

Do you know what your brain does when you are angry? Read the facts below.

BRAIN FACTS

Being mad affects all parts of your brain. Read the facts below to find out how!

1. Your brain is made out of many parts.

2. When you get mad, your brain can release things called "chemicals" and "hormones" into your body that can hurt other organs (like your kidneys).

3. The front part of your brain will change with anger.

4. The middle part of your brain helps you manage stress and helps you create memories. If you stay angry for too long, your brain cannot do this well, and you may also start to feel pain more easily.

5. Stress and being angry affects other parts of your body.

a. Your heart will beat faster and create tighter muscles.

b. You can get sick more often.

c. Your eyes aren't able to see as clearly.

d. You can have trouble eating and maybe get a lot of stomach aches.

e. Your head can hurt more.

f. Your bones can get hurt easier too.

TAKE THE BRAIN FACTS TEST!

Directions: Enter a True or False (T or F) answer to the statements to see how much you remember about what anger can do to your body if you are mad for long periods.

	True	False
1. Being angry for long periods of time does nothing to your body.	☐	☐
2. Anger affects your Brain in many ways.	☐	☐
3. Your Brain has many parts.	☐	☐
4. Anger can hurt the way you remember things.	☐	☐
5. Your kidneys, an organ in your body, are not affected by anger.	☐	☐
6. When angry, you can handle stress better.	☐	☐
7. You might have more problems with stomach aches the more you are angry.	☐	☐
8. Your eyesight can be affected if you are mad a lot.	☐	☐
9. Too much calcium in your brain can take away your ability to plan for things in the future.	☐	☐
10. When you get mad, your brain can hurt your body in some way.	☐	☐

Expressing Anger

Although anger does feel bad, and many people may have an unfavorable view of it, anger actually does serve many good purposes. Expressing your anger is important. When you let go of your anger, you are taking control over your emotions, and that is a great part of being a human!

A few ways anger is helpful for you are:

1. Releasing your anger will help you let go of stress and will help you calm your nerves.

2. Anger can give you energy. Energy can motivate you to do some pretty great things.

3. Anger can help you solve problems. Coming up with new solutions to issues is a great way to focus when you get mad.

4. People find something positive when they get angry. When you get angry about something, it means you care about it. Use that caring feeling to find positivity.

5. Anger can tell you something is wrong. You don't have to act out on it; instead, when you get angry, play detective and figure out what is going on.

EXERCISE 1:
How to Talk about "It"

When you are angry, you may want to yell, scream, hit, kick, or react in some other kind of unhealthy way. Instead, take a moment to recognize that you ARE angry and talk about it with someone. Below is a list of helpful tips that can get the anger out by talking through things.

1. Talk about what makes you angry often.

2. Take a breath before you act.

3. Walk away from what makes you angry.

4. Talk to a mirror — and say, "I'm mad," or "I am angry."

5. Count to ten, then say what is bothering you.

6. Keep your voice low. Keeping a lower voice can relax the muscle tightness anger can bring on.

7. Instead of hitting, kicking, pushing, pulling, etc., speak the words, "I want to hit something." But don't actually do it.

8. Write about your anger right when you are feeling it. Get it out of your head and heart.

9. Find new ways to describe your anger.

10. Give your anger a name (like Tina or Tom).

Now you come up with a few ways to talk about anger. Write them below:

_____

_____

_____

_____

_____

_____

_____

_____

_____

_____

_____

_____

_____

_____

_____

EXERCISE 2:
Learning About Patience

When you're waiting, sometimes it seems like you're going to blow up! But, learning to wait is very helpful and can bring great endings.

Do you know what patience is?

Patience is the ability to wait for something without getting angry or frustrated.

Having patience is definitely hard. But, once you start practicing with it, you can learn to release your anger for so many things. See the items below that can help you learn how to be patient.

Try These Tricks: See What Sticks

1. When something isn't happening quick enough, you can breathe in, then breathe out and count to ten while you're breathing.

2. Each time you feel like you "can't wait!" tell yourself to wait five more seconds.

3. Sing a song when you want something to happen but it seems to be taking too long.

4. Say the alphabet.

5. Spell out the longest states in your country (if in the United States, try Mississippi, Alabama, Montana, California, Pennsylvania, Rhode Island, and more).

6. Think about your favorite movies, TV shows, or books.

7. Think about a new project you can create.

8. Invent something new.

9. Think of how many animals you can name (ex: dog, cat, giraffe, turtle, etc.).

10. Roll some dice and see how many times you can beat your highest number.

Come up with some ideas of your own, write them below!

_____

_____

_____

_____

_____

_____

_____

_____

_____

_____

_____

_____

_____

_____

EXERCISE 3:
Say Something Nice to Yourself

Sometimes when we get angry, it's hard to think of nice things. But, saying just one nice thing to yourself can completely change your mood. See some examples below, and then try to write some ideas down, too, so you have some nice things to say when you are angry at the moment.

I am kind.   _____

I love myself.   _____

I love my family.   _____

I am creative.   _____

I am funny.   _____

I like animals.   _____

I like pets.   _____

I get good grades.   _____

I try my hardest.   _____

I can be a good friend.   _____

                                _____

                                _____

                                _____

                                _____

                                _____

EXERCISE 4:
Say Something Nice to Others

Saying something nice to someone is a great way to relieve your angry feelings. When you get mad, think of something nice to say to the other person. Having a nice thought can defuse angry emotions. See some ideas below and write down things, too, so you have nice views ready.

Thank you for loving me.

Thank you for the help.

You are kind.

I love you.

You are very kind.

EXERCISE 5:
How to Forgive

Learning to forgive is a great way to help yourself as you grow older. When you hold onto anger from things, the anger only grows bigger, which will lead to larger explosions that will be harder to handle when they happen.

Forgiving can feel hard. But when you forgive people, you are permitting yourself to be okay. Here are a few ways to look at forgiveness to help you learn to let things go. Try to write some things down from your mind too.

They probably made a mistake.

There has been a misunderstanding.

They might have been grumpy.

Maybe they were having a bad day.

They would never intentionally hurt me.

EXERCISE 6:
How to Compromise

Compromising is when two ideas come together into one, so it can work for more than one person. Remember, you aren't the only person who wants to have fun or do something, and sometimes you'll need to do things you might not want to do. Learning how to compromise can release your anger—because compromising can help make things better!

Directions: Come up with some compromises for the examples provided below.

EXAMPLE:

Your friend wants to play with action figures, but you want to play a board game.

COMPROMISE _____

_____

EXAMPLE:

Your mom wants you to clean your room. You want to go for a ride around the block on your bike.

COMPROMISE _____

_____

EXAMPLE:

You have to brush your teeth and go to bed, but you aren't tired.

COMPROMISE _____

_____

EXERCISE 7:
Find the Funny

Anger is a strong emotion, but so is humor. When you feel like you are going to explode because you're embarrassed or you made a mistake, turn your anger on its head. Instead, find something funny about the situation.

_____

_____

_____

_____

EXERCISE 8:
Anger Vocabulary

There are different ways that you can get mad. Read the words and the definitions below to help you figure out what kind of anger you have!

Agitated — feeling or appearing troubled or nervous.

Angry — feeling displeased or hostile.

Annoyed — slightly irritated, agitated, frustrated.

Crabby — irritable.

Cranky — ill-tempered, irrational.

Disappointed — sad or displeased because expectations (what you expected to happen) were not met.

Distraught — deeply upset.

Enraged — very angry or furious.

Excitable — responding too quickly to a situation instead of waiting to hear the whole story.

Frustrated — distress and annoyance when there is a change in a situation or an inability to achieve the desired result.

Furious — full of anger, extremely angry. Fury can lead to violence.

Grumpy — irritated or bad mood (usually from a lack of sleep).

Impatient — restless, becomes quickly irritated or easily provoked.

Irritable — have the tendency to be easily annoyed.

Let down — failure to support or be supported by someone as was expected.

Livid — furiously angry.

Mad — very angry.

Offended — insulted by something someone said or did.

Resentful — feeling as though you are being treated unfairly. Bitter about how you feel you have been treated.

EXERCISE 9:
"I" am—Trying to Voice Yourself

When you get mad, sometimes you can't figure out the right way to say things, or sometimes it feels like saying something mean to another person will make you feel better. Neither of those things will help you feel better. Instead, practice using "I" statements. When you reframe what you are saying, you can start to communicate more clearly, which will help you feel like you are being heard.

Try this instead: Take the phrases below and turn them into "I" statements.

EXAMPLE:

You shouldn't have done that!   **"I didn't like what you did."**

YOUR TURN!

You made me angry. _____

Don't do that! _____

Why did you say that? _____

Don't throw that at me! _____

You're not allowed to touch me! _____

Don't look at me. _____

Give that toy back to me! _____

What did you do that for? _____

You are bad! _____

You are mean! _____

NOW THINK ABOUT SOME OF THE THINGS YOU SAY WHEN YOU ARE MAD. WRITE THEM DIFFERENTLY BELOW, REMEMBER TO USE "I" STATEMENTS

_____

_____

_____

_____

_____

_____

_____

_____

_____

_____

_____

_____

_____

_____

_____

EXERCISE 10:
What Happens When You're Angry—The Consequences of Your Angry Actions

Throughout this book, YOU are responsible for your emotions and actions, as we've been saying. Even though you might not be able to control how you feel, you can manage it by not reacting negatively or acting out with anger. Below is a list of consequences if you act out with your anger. After a few of them, write down the consequences of your house too. You can fill this out with your parent or a grown-up who hangs out with you.

Possible Consequences:

Grounded to your room.

No friends.

No video games.

No screen time.

No dessert.

No time to play.

Consequences from Your House Rules

_____

_____

_____

_____

_____

_____

_____

_____

_____

_____

_____

_____

_____

_____

_____

_____

Managing Anger

How to Manage Difficult Feelings

Feelings are good! They let you know what you like and what you don't like. They also give you a chance to learn lessons, grow, and create amazing things. But sometimes, there are times when emotions can be confusing. Anger can be a gauge for letting you know that something is going on you don't like. However, learning how to handle anger in healthy ways can help you figure out the difference between when you don't like what is going on or when you are tired, hungry, or just don't want to follow the rules.

Read and try the exercises below to find new ways to express your anger

EXERCISE 1:
Breathe

As weird as it sounds, breathing is going to help you calm down. Understand that you might still be angry when you are calm, but you won't want to act on that anger. Instead, when relaxed, you can say, "I'm angry. Why?" When you figure out why you're angry, you can develop new solutions to the issue. This means you'll move faster from the unpleasant emotion and into an active role where you can make things better.

Below is a breathing exercise to try when you get angry. You might be surprised at how it works and how much better you'll feel afterward. Once you get used to these breathing exercises, you can do them in many places, so you won't have to sit down and calm yourself at the moment.

Step One

Sit on the floor in a comfortable position.

(You can even ask a grown-up for a pillow to sit on!)

Step Two

Fold your hands.

Step Three

Close your eyes.

Step Four

Breathe in (inhale); as you breathe in, count to four. 1-2-3-4

Step Five

Breathe out (exhale), count to seven.
1-2-3-4-5-6-7

Breathe in and out for three rounds. Then, open your eyes and see how you feel. Write down how your thoughts and feelings changed. Are you still angry? If so, how does the anger feel now? Does it seem less explosive? Can you think better? Are you able to communicate your feelings more clearly? Write your thoughts below.

_____

_____

_____

_____

_____

_____

_____

_____

_____

_____

Try this exercise every day, and once you build up the practice, you can up the number you count to seven as you breathe in (inhale) and ten as you breathe out (exhale).

EXERCISE 2:
Think

When you are done breathing, take the time to think about what you are angry about. You can ask yourself some of the following questions and then come up with some questions of your own to ask.

1. What am I really angry about?

2. Can I do anything about the anger?

3. Can I do anything about the situation that made me mad?

4. What can I do, if I can do anything, about the situation that made me angry?

5. How should I talk to someone about my anger?

6. What would have happened if I acted out on my anger? What would be my consequences?

7. How can I move forward from this anger?

8. How can I let the anger go?

9. What are my next steps?

10. Who can I talk to about my anger?

Now, You ask your questions and write down your responses:

1 _____

_____

2 _____

_____

3 _____

_____

4 _____

_____

5 _____

_____

6 _____

_____

7 _____

_____

8 _____

_____

9 _____

_____

10 _____

_____

After you "Breathe" and "Think," ask yourself one last question — How do I feel Now?

_____

_____

_____

_____

_____

_____

_____

_____

_____

_____

_____

_____

_____

_____

_____

EXERCISE 3:
Listen

When your emotions get strong, chances are you don't want to listen to anyone else. You just want to say stuff. You want to get your anger off your chest and your thoughts out because they are important! But, it's also important to recognize that what other people have to say is important. Everyone deserves a chance to say what they need and want to say.

Many times, we get angry that we misunderstand something that someone said. That is a prime time when listening can be a bonus. If you stop and listen to what the other person is saying, the chances of hearing the entire idea go up 100%. This may stop you from getting angry at all.

Remember to ask questions if you don't understand something the person you are listening to said. Get the full idea, and then you can decide if you don't like what they have to say or not.

Try the exercise below to practice your listening skills, and you can even try these exercises when you are angry.

1. Before you say anything, STOP.

2. Take a breath.

3. Listen to the words the other person is saying.

4. Ask questions about something you don't understand.

5. DECIDE. Do you like what they are saying? Do you understand their side of the story?

6. Tell the other person your thoughts and feelings. Use "I" statements and positive words. Stay away from the "Blame Game."

7. Finally, write or talk about how you handled the situation. If you felt angry, but you did listen, how do you feel about it? Are you proud of yourself? Do you wish you would have said something more? Write down your thoughts and feelings below. Figure out what you can do better next time and what you did well on this time around.

_____

_____

_____

_____

_____

_____

_____

_____

_____

_____

_____

EXERCISE 4:
Reframe

When you start feeling big feelings, your thoughts and words might start to get bigger too. See the examples below on reframing thoughts and ideas that might be exaggerated because of your feelings.

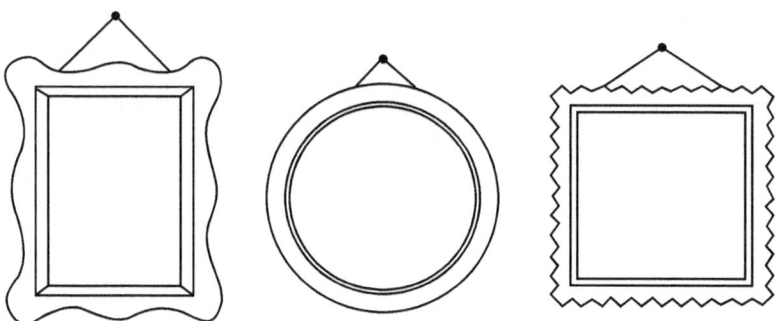

Directions: Review the examples, then use the "instances" to reframe the thought into something more positive. Finally, write down personal examples of when your thoughts and feelings got too big. Try to reframe those "instances" and develop ideas on how they could have been handled differently.

EXAMPLES:

"Instance 1": Someone took the seat I wanted at the dinner table.

"Reframe": It doesn't matter where I sit. I'll still be able to see my family. OR It's okay if they sit next to Mom this time. I'll sit beside her next time.

"Instance 2": I wanted the last piece of chicken, but my older brother took it.

"Reframe": The chicken was so good for dinner it went quickly. I am still hungry, and I should ask for something else to eat.

"Instance 3": I really wanted to eat dessert today. I'm angry because my dad said I couldn't have any.

"Reframe": Dessert would have been nice today. However, if I listen to what my dad says, he will see that I respect him and give me dessert next time.

Now, you try!

"Instance" 1: Danika took the doll I wanted! She ALWAYS takes toys from me.

"Reframe": _____

_____

"Instance" 2: Why do I have to go to bed NOW? I ALWAYS have to go to bed too early.

"Reframe": _____

_____

"Instance" 3: I don't want to eat my food. This food tastes GROSS.

"Reframe": _____

_____

"Instance" 4: I don't like doing homework. It is boring; I am not going to do it.

"Reframe": _____

_____

"Instance" 5: Why do I have to go to the store with my mom? It's so boring, and she doesn't even get me anything.

"Reframe": _____

_____

Now it's Your Turn: Write down a few **"Instances"** that really happened to you, and then come up with how you could have reframed them at the time.

"Instance" 1: _____

_____

_____

_____

"Reframe": _____

_____

_____

_____

"Instance" 2: _____

_____

_____

"Reframe": _____

_____

_____

_____

"Instance" 3: _____

_____

_____

"Reframe": _____

_____

_____

"Instance" 4: _____

_____

_____

"Reframe": _____

_____

_____

"Instance" 5: _____

_____

_____

"Reframe": _____

_____

_____

EXERCISE 5:
Relax

Relaxing may be the last thing you want to do when you're angry. Anger is an emotion that demands action, and instead of kicking, screaming, yelling, hitting, kicking, punching, try to reframe your anger into understanding that relaxing is active too.

How to relax when you are angry:

1. Find a quiet, comfortable place.

2. Try to use your breathing exercises.

3. Focus on any muscles that are tight or in a "fist" (think of how your hands go into a fist when you're angry. Your muscles clench up too). Use your mind to find each tight muscle and then make the tension go away.

    a. Ex: if your hands are in fists, unroll them so they are flat.

    b. Ex: if your teeth are clenched and your jaw is tight, open your mouth and move it around a little.

4. What are your thoughts saying? Just watch the thoughts roll by like clouds.

5. How do you feel after you are relaxed?

EXERCISE 6:
Get Good Sleep

Sleep is a VERY important part of everyday life. If you don't get enough sleep, your brain and body become extra tired, which can make you totally cranky. When you sleep, it clears the toxins out of your brain, and that is a good thing because, as that happens, you will be able to think more clearly, make better choices, and communicate well.

Have a cool-down routine before you go to sleep. About one hour before you go to bed, have special rituals you do with your grown-up. Read a book, journal, listen to quiet music, clean your room, or something more. Having this routine before you go to sleep will help your mind and body wind down, so you are ready to get a good night's sleep, and your brain isn't thinking a whole bunch of thoughts from the day.

Write a cool-down routine below and follow it every night for one month. See if you feel better. If you don't, change it up to have other components. Keep trying until you get the right formula!

EXAMPLE:
1 Hour Before Bed

- Pick up all toys and other objects you've taken out for the day.

- Gather homework and school supplies and put them in your bookbag. Place your bookbag in a specified area.

- Go into your bedroom and straighten anything that needs to be cleared away.

- Turn on relaxing music and change into sleeping clothes.

- Brush teeth and wash your face.

- Climb into bed and read a story.

- Turn light out and relax.

- Fall asleep.

Your Turn:

_____

_____

_____

_____

_____

_____

_____

_____

_____

_____

_____

_____

_____

_____

_____

_____

_____

_____

_____

_____

If the first routine you try doesn't work, change up your routine. But do each change for at least one month to see if it will work.

EXERCISE 7:
Eat Good Food

When you eat good food, you're supplying your brain and body with the best fuel you can. With your body fueled properly, you'll be able to concentrate better, have more energy, and manage your emotions well.

Directions: See the images of food below. Color the good food, and put an X over the bad or unhealthy food. Then talk with your grown-up to learn more about healthier foods.

EXERCISE 8:
Problem Solver—Be the superhero of problems and come up with a new idea

There are times when something doesn't work out the way you want it to. These times can be VERY frustrating, which can also lead to anger. When you find yourself getting angry, the best thing you can do is STOP. THINK. & BREATHE. Once your anger level lowers, you can come up with a new way to do your task and be that superhero problem solver.

Directions: Draw an image of you being a superhero. Think about these questions: What problem are you solving? How did you overcome your frustration and anger? What will you say to yourself to help your anger?

EXERCISE 9:
Trigger Point, Tipping Point

There are going to be times when anger just gets the better of you. It is just going to happen. When it does, it's important to know what triggered your anger and what tipped it off into a full-blown emotion where you reacted in ways that are not healthy ways to respond.

Directions: Write down moments when your anger came around and you didn't manage it in the best way. What happened that started your anger (Trigger Point)? What happened that made your anger spill out everywhere (Tipping Point)? Understanding what happened in those moments will help you manage your anger when similar things creep up.

EXAMPLE:

Trigger Point:

My teacher yelled at me because I was talking in class. She said I ___

___interrupted her lesson. I got embarrassed and angry at myself because of it. _____

Tipping Point:

___I stopped talking, but couldn't get my anger out and as soon as the

___lesson ended, I was going to apologize, but I dropped all my school supplies all over the floor. And I just released my anger out on the first person who said something to me.

Trigger Point: _____

_____

Tipping Point: _____

_____

Trigger Point: _____

_____

Tipping Point: _____

_____

Trigger Point: _____

_____

Tipping Point: _____

_____

Trigger Point: _____

_____

Tipping Point: _____

_____

EXERCISE 10:
Screen-Time and Me Time

Video games, streaming channels, TV, movies, and now even classes or homework can be on screens. The great thing is that screens are VERY helpful in many ways. They can connect you to your family and friends when you miss them but can't be around. And they can entertain or inform you. But, as with everything in life, we need to take some downtime away from even the good things.

The word moderation means: Not doing something in an extreme amount. When you moderate yourself, you are choosing a healthy path. You say that you want to do good things for yourself because you deserve it. Having "Me" time also gives you a chance to know yourself, which is good because you are amazing.

Directions: Come up with 7 activities you can do to spend time with yourself that do NOT include screen time. Then set up a time when you aren't looking at a screen. Also, set time limits on your screen time to ensure that you get to know yourself too.

EXAMPLE:

Take 3 hours for screen time (this includes TV, Movie, Streaming, Social media, and video games). One hour in the morning (not on a school day), 1 after lunch, and 1 hour after dinner.

Activity 1:   Read a book

Activity 2:   Draw, Paint, Color

Activity 3:   Ride my bike

YOUR TURN

Activity 1:

Activity 2:

Activity 3:

Activity 4: _____

_____

_____

Activity 5: _____

_____

_____

Activity 6: _____

_____

_____

Activity 7: _____

_____

_____

Activity 8: _____

_____

_____

Work it Out

Many times, when you are angry, you may have extra energy that will build up so much that the only response is to yell, scream, kick, hit, throw, etc. But angry energy is still energy, and exercising when you are angry is not only healthy for your mind, but for your body too! When you exercise, your brain releases happy brain patterns; they will keep your temper balanced. Try some of the following exercises and see how you feel afterward!

EXERCISE 1:
Jump it Out

Do Jumping Jacks — Do you know how to do jumping jacks? If not, see the image below for help!

Jump Rope — Jumping rope is great fun. You can do it with friends or by yourself. It takes practice, though. Count to see how many times you can jump the rope, and then keep counting to see if you can break your previous record.

Hopscotch — Here is another game you can do by yourself or with others. Plus, you can make new hopscotch boards every time!

1. **Step One:** Draw out a hopscotch board on the ground and number the boxes from 1 to 12 (or higher).

2. **Step Two:** Pick up a pebble.

3. **Step Three:** Throw the pebble onto the hopscotch board. Wherever the pebble lands, you can't jump on that block.

4. **Step Four:** Stand on one foot and jump all the way to 12 (or higher). Try not to fall, and don't jump on the block your pebble is on!

5. **Step Five:** When you get to the end, turn around and go backward 12 to 1. Pick the pebble up on your way back to 1.

Think of other Jumping EXERCISES to do

_____

_____

_____

_____

_____

_____

_____

_____

_____

_____

_____

_____

_____

_____

EXERCISE 2:
Run

- **Run up and down the block.**
- **Run back and forth in your backyard.**
- **Have a race.**
- **Come up with other running games.**

EXERCISE 3:
Ride

Riding bicycles and scooters can be amazing fun. With permission, you can ride around your neighborhood or ask a grown-up to come with you to do even more awesome things like go on a family biking trip, or take your bike to a local park. There are many things to see when you are riding, and it's great exercise. Always remember to follow the rules and stay safe!

EXERCISE 4:
Sports

Sports are another fantastic way to work out and be part of a team. Some sports are ones you can do by yourself too. Plus, there are dozens and dozens of sports to try. The incredible thing about being a kid is that you get to find out what YOU like. This information means you can try out as many things as you want to find what you like the best.

See some sports on the following page, circle the words that sound like you'd like to try them out.

Baseball	Basketball	Football	Cheerleading
Cross Country	Tennis	Golf	Bowling
Pickleball	Raquet Ball	Track	Ice Skating
Roller Skating	Ice Hockey	Lacrosse	Street Hockey
Ping Pong	Skateboarding	Roller Blading	Horseback Riding

Rodeo	Corn Hole	Pool/Billiards	Swimming
Diving	Bocci	Croquet	Badminton
Volleyball	Bike Riding	E-Sports	Surfing
Kayaking	Canoeing	Skiing	Snowboarding

Martial Arts   Fencing   Dodgeball   Kick ball

EXERCISE 5:
Walk it Out

- Go for a walk with a grown-up.
- Go to the park.
- Hike in the woods.
- Walk around the house.
  - Find things
  - Play Eye Spy

Come up with some walking ideas and games to play below:

_____

_____

_____

_____

_____

_____

_____

_____

_____

_____

_____

EXERCISE 6:
Yoga

Yoga is an amazing exercise that will have you stretching out your muscles and joints. Plus, you get some time to quiet your brain and work on letting go of the angry thoughts that may be floating around in your head.

Directions: If you haven't tried yoga before, try the routine below:

Sun Salutations: You'll need comfy clothes and a yoga mat (try a blanket if you do not have a yoga mat).

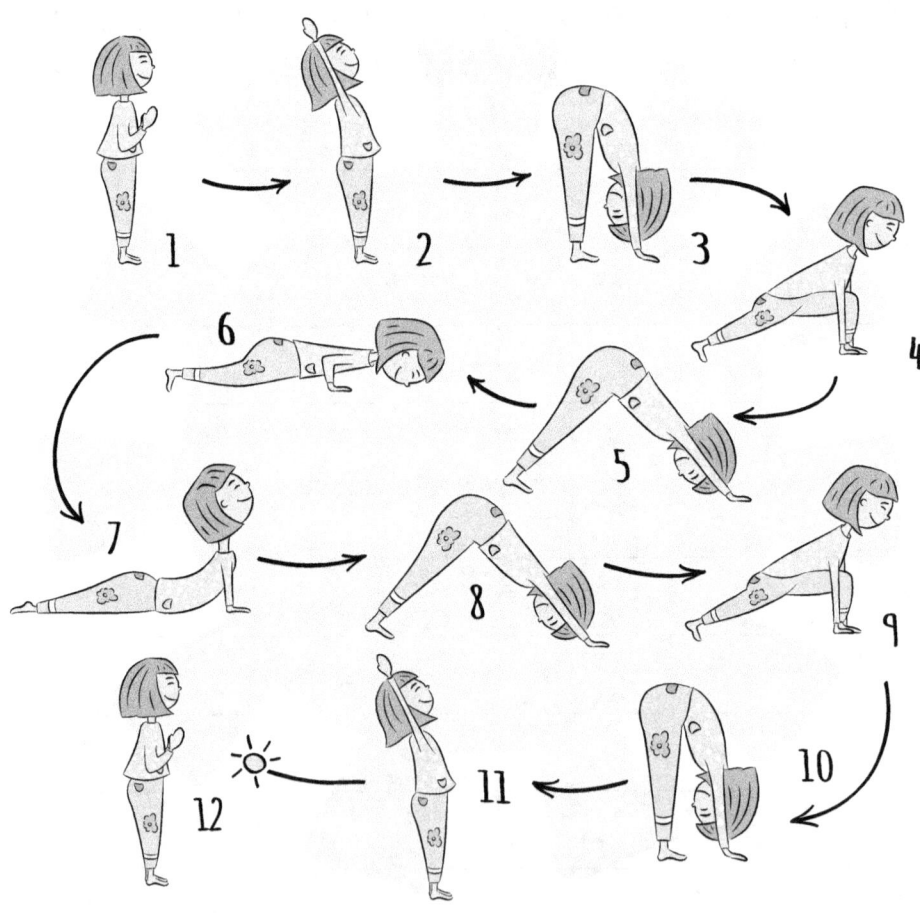

Write about how you feel afterward:

_____

_____

_____

_____

_____

_____

_____

_____

_____

_____

_____

_____

_____

_____

_____

_____

EXERCISE 7:
Dance

Dancing is super fun. It's also a sport, but if you don't want to take dance classes, you don't have to! Instead, put on some music and dance around for at least three songs. Do more if you would like to. Once you start, it's hard to stop!

Directions: Write about some of your favorite music or dance moves below.

_____

_____

_____

_____

_____

_____

_____

_____

_____

Get Creative

Getting creative, especially when you have strong emotions, is a great way to connect with your feelings and get them out of you. Think about the colors of anger. When you get angry, what colors do you see? What colors can you draw? Using your creativity will also give you an active project to do so you can give yourself a break from the big feelings and set yourself apart from what made you mad. See the following exercises and try some of them today!

EXERCISE 1:
Paint, Draw, All Art About it

Finger Paints — Get out some paper and paint and get messy! Put your fingers into the paint and use them instead of your brush. What kind of pictures did you create? (Remember to always get a grown-ups permission first!)

Texture Painting — When you're mad, you may just want to slop some paint on a canvas and call it a day. That's okay! Acrylic paints are the best for this and they dry quickly. You can take a brush and swoosh the paint on your paper or canvas. Or you can just squeeze out the paint from their tubes. Either way, you're entertained, creative, and active.

Drawing with Pencils, Crayons, Markers, and More — There are LOTS of ways to be creative and using some sort of drawing tool (like pencils, chalk, markers, etc.) can be a great way to draw out your feelings.

Tear Some Paper Up — When you get angry, sometimes you just want to rip stuff. That's great energy when you're making a mosaic. Grab some construction paper, rip it up into little bits, then paste it back onto a larger piece of paper and create a great piece of art.

What Other Ways Can You Make Art?

_____

_____

_____

_____

_____

_____

_____

_____

EXERCISE 2:
Make Your Own Stories

Writing is an incredible outlet for creativity and your anger. Write a story below or get a journal to write out your stories, poems, thoughts, and more. See the character's come to life with fiction and find out how you feel better when you get the thoughts and emotions down on paper.

Directions: Write a story below. Use a dragon to represent your anger. Talk about the dragon, and what happens. Are there other characters in the story? How do the characters and the dragon interact? Read your story to someone after you're done writing it!

EXERCISE 3:
Bake it Out

Baking is a nice way to keep your hands busy and your mind occupied while you're sorting through your feelings. Try baking new things and, also, try the marshmallow rice-cereal treat recipe below. You can substitute butters, cereal, and type of marshmallows (vegan or flavored) to combat any food allergies or to just have a treat that tastes different. (Serves 12.)

Equipment:

- Cooking spray
- 9x13 pan
- Glass or metal bowl (or dutch oven)
- Pot of boiling water
- Large bowl
- Mixing Spoons

Ingredients:

- 3 tablespoons of Butter
- 1 ¼ cup of Marshmallows
- 6 cups of Rice Cereal

Instructions:

1. Spray 9x13 pan with cooking spray. Set aside.
2. Melt butter and marshmallows together. You can do this three ways 1) double-boiler, 2) dutch oven, 3) microwave.
   a. Double-Boiler — boil water in a pot, then add glass or metal bowl to the top of the pot, make sure the bowl can sit on top of the pot well. Then, add butter. Then, add marshmallows and melt them together.
   b. Dutch oven — add butter and marshmallows. Melt and mix together.
   c. Microwave butter first. Then add marshmallows; as marshmallows heat, they will get larger, so watch the time — only do it for 20 to 30 seconds at a time. Once the marshmallows have ballooned up, mix them together with the butter.
3. Once melted, add rice cereal to the mixture in a large bowl and stir until all cereal is covered with butter/marshmallow mixture.
4. Add covered rice cereal to 9x13 pan and let the dessert sit until completely cooled.

EXERCISE 4:
Try a New Recipe

Tacos are easy, and you can really get creative. There are meat tacos, fish tacos, vegetarian tacos, dessert tacos, and more! See a quick recipe below for tacos, and you can swap out any ingredients to try new things.

- Taco shells (crunch, soft, or tortilla chips).

- "Stuffings": meats, cheeses, rice, beans, olives, lettuce, fish, shrimp, mushrooms, zucchini, broccoli, strawberries, blueberries, and more!

- If you are cooking meat, fish, beans, rice, or another warm stuffing, make sure that you have a grown-up with you.

- When cutting up other stuffing, make sure that you also have grown-up supervision.

EXERCISE 5:
Try a New Hair Style

- Braiding
- Curling
- Spiking

What other hairstyles can you come up with?

_____

_____

_____

EXERCISE 6:
Crafting

Making A Glitter Jar

Material

- 16-ounce glass or plastic jar that has a lid (mason jars work well)
- Distilled water
- Clear glue
- Corn Syrup
- Glitter or metallic confetti

Instructions

- Pour 8 ounces of distilled water into the jar.
- Add 1 tablespoon of corn syrup.
- Add 1 tablespoon of clear glue.
- Add 1/4 cup of glitter.
- Pour rest of the water into the jar.
- Tighten lid (you can seal the lid with hot or super glue).
- Shake the glitter jar up and watch it.

EXERCISE 7:
Make a Calm Place

Find a spot in your house that is just for you. Every time you get mad, go to the spot and feel your feelings. What's great is that with your grown-up's help, you can decorate it to encourage a calm feeling when you get there.

EXAMPLE

A nook in the house can have a special scent, low lighting, and pictures of calming things (ocean, forest, etc.). Add your stuffed animals, blankets, radio, or more.

Write down a list of items you would like to add to your distraction box too:

_____

_____

_____

_____

EXERCISE 8:
Create a Distraction Box

When you are angry, sometimes you need a distraction. Why not create a box that has special items in it to keep you entertained when you are mad? You can even decorate the distraction box with a bunch of your favorite things.

EXAMPLE

Box of cards, dice, book, a blanket with your favorite scent on it, and journal.

Write down a list of items you would like to add to your distraction box too:

_____

_____

_____

_____

_____

_____

_____

_____

_____

Extras

EXERCISE 1:
Clean

Cleaning may not sound like fun, but it does help with anger. You don't even have to clean a big spot; just take a small task or project on when you're angry. You'll be surprised at how quickly you'll start to feel better.

EXERCISE 2:
Organize

Like cleaning, organizing sounds more like a chore than anything else. But, when you have a clear and organized space, your mind is clear and organized too. After you arrange a small spot in your room or another place in the house, you'll be able to have time to think about your anger and communicate it more clearly to someone, which will make you feel better.

EXERCISE 3:
Quiet Time

Spend 20 minutes to an hour in a calm place or lie in bed until your feelings relax a little. Give yourself time to think about your feelings. Doing this for yourself will help you better understand new parts of yourself and give you a healthy outlet for your anger.

EXERCISE 4:
Find Gratitude

Being thankful for things in your life can help calm any strong feelings like anger. Think about three things you're grateful for and write them down. Each time you get angry, you can think of the same things or find new things to be thankful for.

EXAMPLE

Friends, Family, House, Food

YOUR TURN

_____

_____

_____

_____

_____

Goodbye, Anger

EXERCISE 1:
Where Does Your Anger Go?

It's important to know that the anger goes away once you feel your feelings and work through them. However, if you don't go all the way through, there may be some lingering anger about what triggered your emotions. Don't be surprised if it takes a little time to master going through your anger, but you can get there.

EXERCISE 2:
Your Thoughts and Feelings After Anger

How do you feel after you get angry? What are your thoughts? Write down these things to see if you've gotten through your feelings or if there is still something to work through. Also, check your thoughts. Sometimes angry emotions bring angry or unhealthy ideas. You're going to want to say one nice thing to yourself (about yourself!) at the end of this writing session.

Directions: Write your thoughts and feelings below.

_____

_____

_____

_____

_____

_____

_____

_____

_____

_____

_____

_____

_____

_____

_____

_____

_____

_____

_____

_____

_____

_____

EXERCISE 3:
Other People and Your Anger, After Your Anger is Gone

You may have to talk to someone or some people after you've gotten angry or done something to them when you got angry. Speaking to someone after you've treated them with your angry feelings can be difficult, but it's important to show them that you care. You can practice below at saying some nice or apologetic things to get an idea of how to communicate with others.

EXAMPLE 1

I am sorry I lost my temper at you.

EXAMPLE 2

I am sorry I hurt your feelings.

EXAMPLE 3

I could have listened to what you said better.

NOW YOU TRY:

_____

_____

_____

_____

_____

_____

Conclusion

Now that you've made your way through the workbook, you have the knowledge and tools to keep helping yourself when you get mad. Great Job! You are the master of your emotions and can choose to react to your anger, or you can do some of the fun activities you've learned.

Just because you've finished the workbook doesn't mean that you can't come back to it when you're feeling angry, overwhelmed, or forget some key activity you'd like to do again.

Remember to talk to your parents, grandparents, and caregivers when you have big feelings. Letting them out of your mind and heart will help you let go of things easier and help you not feel like you're going to blow up every once in a while. But remember to be kind to yourself when you do blow up. Breathe, Think, Reset, Reframe. You can do it. You are amazing!

Michael B. Stump
The Mentor Bucket

Free Bonus

For being our valued customer, we wanted to offer you our 3 reports absolutely FREE...

HOW TO TEACH KIDS TO IDENTIFY & DEAL WITH THEIR **ANGER TRIGGERS**

FREE REPORT

THE MENTOR BUCKET

5 THINGS PARENTS NEED TO KNOW ABOUT **TANTRUMS** ....AND HOW TO STOP THEM!

FREE REPORT

THE MENTOR BUCKET

HOW PARENTS MAKE THEIR **CHILD ANGER WORSE** (...WITHOUT KNOWING IT) **& WHAT TO DO INSTEAD!**

FREE REPORT

THE MENTOR BUCKET

Download these reports by scanning the code!

(Your Mobile Camera Has A Built In Scanner.)

SCAN ME